Original title:
Trellis of Truth

Copyright © 2025 Creative Arts Management OÜ
All rights reserved.

Author: Oliver Bennett
ISBN HARDBACK: 978-1-80566-601-1
ISBN PAPERBACK: 978-1-80566-886-2

Blooming in Transparency

In the garden of gossip, blooms taunt,
Funny whispers sprout, we all just want.
Bright petals giggle, in sunlight's glare,
Honesty's flower, spread everywhere.

Bumblebees buzz to the tale they weave,
Pollen of laughter, you wouldn't believe.
Each stem a secret, each leaf a jest,
Transparent blooms, oh how they're blessed.

Embracing the Honest Blossom

Among the blooms, a laugh takes flight,
Sunshine chuckles, and shadows feel light.
Petals tickle, buds start to sway,
In this honest garden, we play all day.

Fragrant truths dance in the summer breeze,
Jokes grow wild like vines on trees.
With every blossom, a wink and a grin,
Honesty's fun, let the games begin!

The Network of Nuanced Narratives

A web of tales spun fine as silk,
Each thread a story, smooth as milk.
Tangled narratives tickle the mind,
In laughter's embrace, joy you will find.

Whimsical whispers behind every leaf,
Secrets that spark, never bring grief.
Threads connecting, weaving the jest,
In this quirky tale, we're surely blessed.

Secrets Beneath the Surface

Beneath the soil, where the gnomes reside,
Lies a treasure of giggles and secrets wide.
Worms are the messengers, funny and sly,
Uncovering wonders that make you cry.

With every shovel, a joke may emerge,
Laughter erupts, an unstoppable surge.
Roots intertwine, creating a show,
In this secret garden, enjoy the flow!

The Density of Heartfelt Revelations

In a garden of giggles, thoughts sprout,
Like weeds in a lawn, they wiggle about.
We dig for the truth, so cleverly wrapped,
In layers of laughter, we've happily napped.

Eureka, we shout, as we flip through the dirt,
Uncovering secrets, while hiking in flirt.
The soil of our hearts, a comedic affair,
Where chuckles bloom freely, floating in air.

The Espalier of Introspection

In narrow confines, our thoughts are strung,
Like peas in a pod, where the wisecracks are sung.
Each branch a dilemma, each leaf a quirk,
We prune with a grin, as we giggle at work.

The structure is wobbly, a bit out of line,
Yet wisdom grows sideways, just give it some time.
With lopsided balance, we laugh at the mess,
As reason dangles precariously, I confess.

Ribbons of Raw Reflection

Tangled up thoughts, like spaghetti on plates,
In the kitchen of life, where humor awaits.
We stir a big pot of introspective stew,
A dash of absurd, and a pinch of the true.

As the ribbons unwind, they dance in a twirl,
A comedy show in this life's crazy whirl.
Each twist and each turn, a silliness found,
In the depths of our minds, where laughter abounds.

The Tapestry of Honest Growth

We weave with delight, our truths in a mesh,
Each thread is a giggle, a lighthearted flesh.
Stitching up honesty, one weave at a time,
With needles of humor, our laughter's the rhyme.

As patterns emerge, wild stories take flight,
Our fabric of folly grows thicker each night.
In the loom of our lives, we twist and we play,
Crafting tales of absurdity, day after day.

From Roots to Revelations

Roots that wiggle, dance around,
Spreading secrets underground.
Leaves overhead, knock-knock jokes,
Witty whispers from leafy folks.

The sun chuckles, casting rays,
While shadows play in silly ways.
Digging deep for laughter's gold,
A garden tale that's never old.

The Arch of Authenticity

Beneath the arch, quirks abound,
Spilling truths in laughter's sound.
Wobbly bricks of honest glee,
Whispering what it means to be.

Joke-laden vines entwining tight,
Giggling stars in the moonlight.
With each blossom, a punchline new,
Growing joy, that's what we do.

Cultivating the Light Within

Plant a seed of humor bright,
Water with giggles, let it ignite.
Digging deep, we find the glow,
Sprouting laughs, see how they flow.

Fertilize the soil with cheer,
Pull weeds of doubt, draw near.
Nurtured well, the smiles bloom,
Filling hearts, dispelling gloom.

In the Heart of the Bloom

In the bloom where laughter grows,
Tickled petals, soft and close.
Funny bees come buzzing round,
In this garden, joy is found.

Silly stems in vibrant hues,
Dance with every breeze that cues.
Nature's jesters, bright and spry,
Winking blooms catch every eye.

The Archway of Open Dialogues

In a garden where whispers bloom,
Chit-chatting over a pickle jar,
We debate if cucumbers feel,
And does laughter travel far?

The puns hang low on the clothesline,
Where socks have dreams of being stars,
We argue whether cats can talk,
And if sandwiches know who we are.

An echo of giggles flits about,
As frogs critique the sun's bright rays,
In the shade, we craft new jest,
About fish that dance on sunny days.

Beneath the arch, truths twist and turn,
Like spaghetti in a chef's wild dance,
We stumble on unknown ideas,
And share our thoughts with a silly glance.

The Quiet Embrace of Wisdom

There's a cat with wisdom in its meow,
Who gives advice on how to nap,
It claims that dreams are just a show,
And life's a game of mischievous clap.

With pillows stacked in wonky style,
We ponder why socks always flee,
And laugh at birds that seem to smile,
As if they're sharing coffee with me.

The wise old owl gives a shrug,
When asked for secrets he'll not share,
Instead he offers a cozy hug,
And reminds us life's a playful affair.

In evenings wrapped in quiet cheer,
We sip on tea and plan our schemes,
With cozy wisdom drawing near,
Life's best lived between the dreams.

Branches of Trust in Bloom

Branches sway with jokes unspoken,
Where squirrels plot their nutty heist,
And acorns giggle, slightly broken,
As trust grows thicker than morning mist.

We gather round in leafy shade,
As giggles bounce from tree to tree,
Sharing secrets, trust conveyed,
Like bees that dance so wild and free.

With every rustle, tales unfold,
Of missed connections, silly slips,
In this forest, brave and bold,
Where friendship blooms in carefree quips.

And so we climb, on branches high,
Tracking laughter through the leaves,
Where every fall is worth a try,
In trust's embrace, the heart believes.

The Framework of Reality

In a world made of noodles, life slurps up tight,
With spaghetti-like thoughts that dance in the night.
Wobbling truths hang like socks on a line,
Where dreams come to dry, oh so funny, so fine!

We build our own castles with bricks of delight,
While pigeons coo secrets that take to flight.
In a frame of confusion, we craft our own play,
With laughter our guide, we'll twirl night and day.

Growth in the Shade

Under the beans that twist and embrace,
My sense of direction has lost its old grace.
With shadows that giggle and roots that tease,
I laugh with the leaves in the mild summer breeze.

Where cucumbers joke about heights they can't reach,
And tomatoes give speeches on sweet, juicy speech.
In the garden of whimsy, we sprout and we sway,
With chuckles and grins lighting up our bouquet.

Blossoms of Unspoken Wonder

Petals are whispering of secrets untold,
As daisies collect stories from marigold mold.
In this patch of nonsense, we twirl and we spin,
While butterflies giggle, inviting us in.

With flowers that wink and a breeze that sighs,
We gather our jokes under vast, open skies.
In the garden of chuckles, ridiculous and free,
We plant seeds of laughter, so wide-eyed they be.

In the Lattice of Insight

Through the grid of our musings, a riddle takes form,
Like socks in the dryer, we tumble, we swarm.
Every twist holds a punchline, each turn has a jest,
In the maze of our minds, absurdity's best.

We navigate tangles of thoughts gone awry,
Where quips roll like marbles that fumble and fly.
With laughter as fuel, our wisdom expands,
In a lattice of giggles, we craft life's demands.

Harmony Among the Roots

In the garden of giggles, roots intertwine,
Tangles of laughter, oh, how they shine.
Worms share their secrets, plants hum a tune,
Sunflowers dancing, under a bright moon.

Beneath leafy whispers, wise squirrels conspire,
Chasing their tails, as if stuck in a liar.
Buds blink with wonder, as they bloom and they fade,
In this silly jungle, truth wears a charade.

Growth of Genuine Discourse

Words sprout like daisies, so cheerful and bright,
Conversations unfold in the warm morning light.
Chatterbox bees buzz, with stories to trade,
Frogs croak opinions, never afraid.

Vines tangled in jest, climbing up every wall,
Each quip and each pun, a fun little brawl.
The roots roll their eyes, in a comical dance,
Daring each other to give joy a chance.

The Canopy of Concealed Meaning

Beneath thick branches, where shadows reside,
Words play hide and seek, trying to abide.
The owls hoot softly, with wisdom to share,
In riddles and puns, the meaning is rare.

Chipmunks debate, with a flick of their tails,
Spinning wild tales, like winds in the gales.
Secrets woven tightly, laughter takes flight,
A canopy ponders through day and through night.

Interwoven Moments of Clarity

In the tapestry of folly, moments unwind,
Each stitch a chuckle, a lively rewind.
Butterflies flap, with jokes they relay,
Sprinkling humor, in a whimsical way.

Caterpillars giggle, they wiggle and sway,
While shadows discuss, what trees had to say.
Connections like vines, so silly yet bright,
In this woven chaos, truth giggles in flight.

Layers of Genuine Dialogue

In layers thick like grandma's pie,
We patch our thoughts both low and high.
With words like marshmallows, soft and sweet,
Our chats are tasty, a real treat!

We mix our stories, stir the pot,
A recipe for laughs, quite hit or not.
Like onions peel, we shed a tear,
But jokes flow freely, no need to fear.

Beneath the surface, giggles churn,
In every pause, new lessons learn.
A secret sauce of trust we blend,
To spice our talks, they never end!

So gather round for fun and cheer,
Through layers deep, our truths appear.
We navigate with humor's guide,
In dialogue's dance, we take a ride!

The Cloister of Clear Insights

In cloisters where the jesters play,
We share insights in a silly way.
A riddle here and a pun right there,
In laughter's arms, we strip off care.

With quirky hats and goofy grins,
We find the truth where humor spins.
A trumpet blast of witty schemes,
To wake the mind from daytime dreams!

Each thought's a kite, we let them fly,
With laughter's wind, they touch the sky.
A festival of funny lights,
In clarity's glow, we see the sights!

So come and join this merry throng,
In cloisters bright, we sing the song.
With insights clear and hearts so bold,
A tapestry of laughter told!

The Maze of Mutual Understanding

In a maze of thoughts, we twist and turn,
With each wrong bend, our heads we'll churn.
But giggles echo through the walls,
As friendly banter softly calls.

Around the corner, you'll find me there,
With pie on my face, but none will stare.
For in this maze, we're pals and pals,
Unraveling laughs in playful gales!

Each sentence fragrant, like fresh-baked bread,
Filling the space, no fear or dread.
With humor's compass, we find our way,
Through twists and turns, we laugh and play!

So hold my hand, let's wander wide,
In mutual minds, we take in stride.
With joyful hearts and minds so free,
In the maze of thought, is you and me!

The Clarity in Shadows

In shadows deep where giggles hide,
We find clarity, side by side.
A whispered joke, a knowing grin,
In laughter's glow, the fun begins!

With flashlights bright, we chase the dark,
Unraveling shadows with a spark.
Like cats, we pounce on silly fears,
With every chuckle, laughter clears.

Through twists and quirks, we find our way,
In silly dances, our minds at play.
With every jest, new visions bloom,
In shadows bright, there's no more gloom!

So join the quest for laughs and fun,
In clarity's light, we've just begun.
With hearts so light, we'll take the leap,
In joyful shadows, our secrets keep!

Ties of Trust and Transparency

In a world where secrets hide,
The cat's out, no need to slide.
With laughter shared, we all can see,
The jokes on us, oh woe is me!

Knots we tie, both firm and loose,
Like friendships built, a joyful truce.
Tangled webs and giggles sprout,
In trust we laugh, without a doubt.

Silly whispers, bonds so tight,
You share your cake, I'll take a bite.
Transparent tales of goofy glee,
Is this true, or just a spree?

So hand in hand, we skip along,
With silly songs, we all belong.
In this dance of trust, let's prance,
And take a chance on happenstance!

Canopy of the Soul's Clarity

Underneath the leafy shade,
Truths will flourish, unafraid.
Beneath the layers, we unearth,
That laughter's worth is more than mirth.

Clouds above might drift and sway,
But honesty's a silly play.
Shiny sunbeams peek and poke,
With silly jokes that make us choke.

When ego's out, the jesters start,
As clarity tickles each heart.
Like squirrels up there, we plan to climb,
In this tree of life, we lose all time.

So let's frolic, twirl, and dance,
In this canopy, we take a chance.
With each chuckle, we'll all grow,
In soul's clarity, let truth bestow!

Frames of Inner Truths

Picture frames and silly frowns,
Painted smiles and upside-downs.
In canvas clear, the jokes unfold,
Revealing truths that weren't so bold.

Snap a shot, oh what a sight,
Silly moments, pure delight.
Each frame a tale, both odd and wack,
In laughter's grip, we won't look back.

Puzzle pieces, one by one,
Aligning shapes till we are done.
With each mistake, we'll laugh and cheer,
Framed in joy, no need for fear.

So gather 'round this merry crew,
In these frames, find something new.
The art of truth is truly sweet,
In laughter's dance, we're all complete!

The Weave of Life's Mysteries

Threads of fate all intertwine,
Life's a tapestry, oh so fine.
With colorful patterns, wild and bright,
Each twist and turn brings pure delight.

Bumpy roads and silly bends,
Patterns shift as laughter blends.
With every knot, a tale is spun,
In the weave of life, we're all for fun.

Yarns of wisdom, a crazy loom,
Twisting truth with joy to bloom.
Each frayed edge tells a story,
In messy stitches, find the glory.

So let the weavers take a stand,
With giggles shared, let's make a band.
In life's great weave, let's dance and cheer,
For mysteries wrapped in laughter near!

Canopy of Clarity

Under leafy puns so bright,
We giggle as we take flight.
A canopy that tells no lies,
With truths that wear a funny guise.

The beans we spill are light as air,
Wrapped in laughter everywhere.
Sunshine tickles all our frowns,
While joy flips old sad clowns upside down.

In this grove, we plant our quirks,
The bark is soft, and fun just lurks.
We tickle each unspoken thought,
And laugh at truths that once were caught.

So join this dance beneath the leaves,
We'll spin the tales that no one grieves.
In this shade, let laughter bloom,
So glorious, it dispels all gloom.

The Framework of Honesty

A frame of jokes that's built so fine,
With humor woven like a vine.
Each corner holds a silly grin,
Where truths and giggles dance within.

The beams are made of playful chat,
Hanging hats and coats, oh, imagine that!
We build a house of trust and cheer,
Where honesty can disappear.

Wobbly stools and wobblier tales,
Like ships set sail on windy gales.
A riddle here, a pun there too,
In this structure, laughter grew.

So grab a tool, let's craft our fun,
A framework built for everyone.
Together let's make this place a hoot,
Where laughs and truths are absolute.

When Flowers Speak in Colors

Petals giggle in vibrant hues,
Their jokes are sweeter than morning dew.
With every bloom, a whispered quip,
In garden beds, the colors flip.

Sunflowers wink with golden light,
While daisies dance, oh what a sight!
Roses blush and share a jest,
A bouquet of hilarity shares its quest.

Lilies laugh in gentle grace,
Their tales of mischief fill the space.
In this landscape, humor grows,
As blossoms gossip, everyone knows.

So let them chatter, let them play,
In colors bright, they light the way.
With every bloom, a smile unfurled,
A garden full of jokes is twirled.

Beneath the Blossoms' Veil

Beneath the blooms where secrets hide,
Lies a world of laughter tied.
Petals whisper, giggles flow,
In this haven, joy will grow.

With vines that twist and tickle too,
They share their tales just me and you.
Underneath their colorful care,
Lies a truth that's light and rare.

The branches nod, the laughter swells,
In this grove, each joke compels.
Floral frolics dance about,
In this curtain, fun's no doubt.

So take a seat beneath this shade,
Where laughter's song will never fade.
With every rustle, joy unveils,
In the heart of blossoms' tales.

Secrets Entwined in Greenery

In gardens where the gnomes reside,
Whispers bounce with a playful stride.
The daisies giggle, the roses grin,
While snails debate who'll win the spin.

Underneath the creeping vine,
Lies a secret, oh so fine!
A squirrel steals an acorn or two,
While a robin plots its next debut.

The caterpillars dance in line,
Swinging low on threads divine.
Worms exchange their latest news,
As the daisies share their favorite blues.

In every bush and leafy nook,
There's a tale that begs a look.
With laughter filling up the air,
Nature's jest, a joyful affair.

The Web of Wise Understanding

Spiders spin their brilliant threads,
Telling tales like artistic leads.
Each shine reveals a clever riddle,
While ants argue over the fiddle.

The bees buzz in a humming choir,
With gossip that never tires.
They chat about the flowers' hues,
And how to score the finest views.

A wise old owl hoots at the dawn,
Keenly watching the lawn.
He chuckles softly in delight,
At foxes sneaking for a bite.

In nature's theater, there's no case,
Where laughter doesn't find its place.
So tread lightly on paths unseen,
And join the dance of greenery's scene.

Insights Through the Leaves

Leaves converse, rustling soft tones,
Exchanging tales of their tiny clones.
The sun peeks through, a playful tease,
While shadows giggle amongst the trees.

Squirrels chatter, plotting their schemes,
While frogs croak on their leafy dreams.
A wisecracking crow steals the show,
With punchlines only he would know.

The blooms nod with a fragrant grin,
As vines intrude with a subtle spin.
Nature's wit in the breeze so clear,
Invites all to lend an ear.

With every sway, there's joy to find,
In secrets told by roots entwined.
For laughter echoes in the glade,
A jubilee in leaf parade.

The Arch of Unfolding Truth

Under arches made of twine,
Secrets bloom and jokes align.
A peppered parrot squawks in mirth,
As the slugs launch their new rebirth!

The laughter of leaves fills the air,
While rabbits plot without a care.
They hop around with a sprightly skip,
In this curious garden trip.

A dog barks out a comic sound,
Chasing shadows around and round.
With every turn, a grin they wear,
These funny friends without a care.

The arch stands proud in this leafy play,
As wisdom unfolds in a witty way.
In every sound, a chuckle grows,
In laughter's embrace, the truth bestows.

Harbingers of Hopeful Honesty

In the garden of whispers, secrets take flight,
The gnomes hold meetings, under the moonlight.
They giggle and chuckle, at truths yet untold,
As daisies eavesdrop, their petals unfold.

A squirrel named Larry, with wisdom so bold,
Claims honesty's candy is worth its weight gold.
But when asked for a taste, he just shrugs and grins,
Turns out his sweet lies are made of old skins!

With worms in attendance, they all raise a cheer,
For honest confessions, they hold ever dear.
Yet when no one's watching, they snicker and jest,
At truths thinner than air, it's all quite the test.

So the flowers keep nodding, through sunbeams and shade,
At children of honesty, in games they have played.
The gnomes declare victory, as laughter takes root,
In a world full of fables, the fun's absolute!

Pergola of Unmasked Feelings

Beneath a pergola, where feelings convene,
A potpourri of laughter, in shades evergreen.
The vines wrap around, with hugs they provide,
But one cheeky fern just refuses to hide.

It screams, 'I'm a cactus, with feelings so grand!
I prick when I'm poked, this no one can stand!'
The daisies all giggle, while rolling in glee,
At this prickly fellow, who can't see he's free.

The butterflies flutter, in swirling delight,
As secrets of blossoms take beautiful flight.
Each petal a whisper, of love and some woe,
Yet everyone knows, it's just for the show.

So laughter erupts in a floral ruckus,
With daisies in crowns, they sing out a fuss.
The cactus rolls over, in fits of surprise,
Who knew that such banter could burst with such lies!

Unraveled Threads of Existence

In a world woven tight with thoughts quite astute,
A weaver named Frank, he's slightly off-route.
His yarns twist and tangle, yet hold a great charm,
While knitting a tale with his bright purple farm.

He drops all his stitches, declares, 'What a mess!
But what's life without laughter? Must I confess!'
Cotton and wool, they dance in delight,
As the threadbare truths come unraveled by night.

With a spool full of giggles, and a needle of fate,
He stitches up nonsense that's genuinely great.
"Life's but a wobbly, whimsical show,"
He shouts with a grin, "Let's give it a go!"

So the fabric of living, though frayed at the seams,
Turns vibrant with color, fulfill all your dreams.
For each tangled tale, though it seems to be brash,
Ends with a punchline, and laughter's the crash!

The Interlace of Intention and Insight

In a café of thoughts, where intentions collide,
A barista named Jane serves espresso with pride.
She brews up some insight, with a wink and a grin,
Saying, "Life's just a blend, now let's pour it in!"

The customers chuckle, as each cup they embrace,
With froth-topped theories, they sip and they race.
"I swear, my latte knows exactly my heart,
It whispers sweet hints, where should I start?"

With sprinkles of nonsense, the table erupts,
Quite like an engine that just cannot stop.
For intention's a jester, insight plays games,
In a circus of laughter, with truth's funny names.

So sip on adventures, let worries dissolve,
For each cup tells a story, that we must involve.
As Jane grins away, in her caffeinated bliss,
She knows every truth comes with a humorous twist!

The Framework of Sincerity

In a garden, truths are pruned,
Giggling leaves sing out loud.
A fence of honesty is strewn,
With daisies making us proud.

The rabbits dance, a silly sight,
With secrets shared through vines.
They jump and twirl with pure delight,
In a maze of laughter lines.

Bumblebees buzz with bright intent,
As whispers float from rose to rose.
The breeze, a jest, it's heaven-sent,
As honesty in jest often grows.

So let's all laugh beneath the sun,
In this garden of true absurdity.
Together, we will have such fun,
In the framework of pure sincerity.

Ferns and Fragments of Fact

Amidst the ferns, the facts will bloom,
In shapes that twist and twirl.
With silly shadows adding room,
For laughter's light to swirl.

Fragments shared by quirky birds,
Who chirp with comedic flair.
Their stories flip like playful words,
Floating gently through the air.

A squirrel boasts of acorn quests,
While leaves giggle, bright and keen.
In this realm of funny tests,
The truths are rarely what they seem.

So come and join, let's weave and sprout,
In ferns, our simple plan.
With laughter loud, there's naught to doubt,
In fragments, we all understand.

Nature's Web of Understanding

In nature's web, we twist and turn,
With jests that tickle, twist, and tease.
The questions dance, and hearts will yearn,
For wisdom found upon the breeze.

The spiders spin their tales of yarn,
Each thread a giggle, each knot a glee.
Around the flowers, truth will charm,
As knowledge sways, wild and free.

With laughter bouncing like a ball,
The birds convene to share the fun.
In this web where giggles call,
We find our wits before we run.

So gather 'round, in joy we stand,
Beneath the sun's warm, golden ray.
Together we'll weave, hand in hand,
In nature's web, come what may.

The Climbing Roses of Knowing

The climbing roses stretch and sway,
With petals soft and color bright.
They laugh as truths come out to play,
In hues of red and pure delight.

A bumblebee trips on the vine,
As witty whispers fill the air.
Its buzz a song that feels divine,
While secrets dance without a care.

Each thorn a joke, each bloom a jest,
In this garden, no one's better.
With snickers shared among the rest,
We find our hearts shaped like a letter.

So let's lift out glasses and toast,
To roses bold in their knotted show.
In joy and laughter, we will boast,
The climbing roses help us grow.

Weaving the Path of Integrity

In a garden full of whines,
The carrots dance, the grapevine twines.
Tomatoes tell tales of woe,
While radishes play peek-a-boo, you know!

A cabbage wears a crown of leaves,
Speaking wisdom no one believes.
The peas roll laughter on the ground,
As integrity's roots go round and round.

With each step among the greens,
Truth wears a pair of silly jeans.
Why should the turnips keep a frown,
When beans will always come around?

So let's plant seeds with joyful cheer,
In this patch, honesty volunteers.
Laughing as we share our plight,
Weaving a path of pure delight.

Reflections in the Dew

Morning light on lilac limbs,
Dewdrops glisten like silly hymns.
A rabbit hops, then spins around,
Chasing shadows that can't be found.

Each droplet holds a tiny tale,
Of whispering winds and goofy gales.
The daisies chuckle, saying, 'Look!'
As the sun peeks in like a friendly nook.

While ferns fold up in laughter's grace,
A snail slides in, it's quite the race.
Who knew that slugs could have such style?
In the garden, we all share a smile.

So let's drink in this morning brew,
Finding joy in each bright view.
Through laughter, we start the day anew,
In nature's play, we find our clue.

Between the Stems of Perception

In the patch where wildflowers bloom,
Perception weaves a vibrant loom.
Butterflies waltz on a whim,
As bees sync up to a happy hymn.

At times they argue, right and wrong,
While ladybugs hum a tuneless song.
A wise old owl, perched up high,
Squirrels jest as they scamper by.

Each stem holds secrets of laugh and cheer,
Telling tales that all can hear.
The blooms wink knowingly at the bees,
While mischief dances on the breeze.

So stop and peek between the green,
Where giggles dwell and quirks are seen.
In the fields of thought, don't be shy,
Let perceptions bloom, and laughter fly!

Echoes in the Wildflowers

Wildflowers whisper in the breeze,
Tickling thoughts with playful tease.
Sunshine peeks through foliage bright,
Casting giggles in golden light.

A dandelion makes a wish,
Chasing clouds like a goofy fish.
While crickets chirp a funny tune,
The stars giggle and wink at the moon.

In the meadow, every color sings,
As laughter hops on playful wings.
From buttercups to violets' grace,
Even weeds wear a smile on their face.

So join the echoes, dance along,
In wildflower realms, we all belong.
With every step, let joy unfurl,
In nature's song, we twirl and whirl!

Shelter of Shared Realities

Under the sneeze of tangled lies,
We laugh at echoes, no need for ties.
A fence of whispers, a wall of cheer,
Hiding our secrets, oh dear, oh dear!

Beneath the trees, we play charades,
Dancing on paths where reason fades.
The sun gets lost in our belly laughs,
While shadows play our silly drafts.

With tea made strong and stories tall,
We weave our tales, a tangled sprawl.
Reality's cousin, just out of sight,
Grins at the nonsense, riding the night.

When truths collide, we just take flight,
On kites of giggles, up, up, we light.
In this shared shelter, we all belong,
A playful choir, a joyful song.

The Garden Path of Truthfulness

In a garden filled with tangled weeds,
We plant our daisies, share our seeds.
Truths sprout funny, like beans on toast,
Wobbling wildly, we giggle the most.

With laughter stitched into our rows,
We pluck the carrots where nothing grows.
Who knew a bloom could wear such a hat?
As bees make honey, we sit and chat.

The sun takes breaks, the clouds have fun,
As we race shadows, just trying to run.
With every slip on this bumpy trail,
We find a punchline, we cannot fail.

In a world of blooms, both grand and small,
We dance on the paths, yes, we bring it all.
Truth may be funny, absurd or spry,
But in this garden, we let it fly.

Veils of Vivid Awareness

In a world where colors blend and swirl,
We paint our truths with a mischievous whirl.
Foggy spectacles, topsy-turvy shades,
We giggle at the truth as it quickly fades.

Awareness flutters like a silly bird,
Each flap a secret, each song absurd.
Dressed in rainbows, we chase the clues,
While wisdom plays hopscotch in mismatched shoes.

A veil of laughter wraps around the day,
As we juggle honesty in a playful way.
Truths sneaking out like a cat on a wall,
We wave them goodbye, they go with a sprawl.

In this vivacious dance of clueless delight,
We stumble on answers hidden from sight.
And as the colors fade into the night,
We cherish our veils, they feel just right.

Whispers in the Wilderness

In the wild where giggles echo vast,
Whispers bounce back, we are unsurpassed.
A rabbit's chuckle, a squirrel's grin,
Each rustling leaf hides the fun within.

Tangled paths lead us on silly quests,
Hopping from truth to playful jest.
A fox in sneakers, a bear who sings,
Welcome to nature where nonsense springs.

With branches weaving a canopy dense,
We plot our mischief, it all makes sense.
While mushrooms chuckle and owls roll their eyes,
The wilderness laughs, it's full of surprise.

So here we wander, hand in hand,
In a funny realm, the grandest stand.
Whispers of joy float through the trees,
In this wild embrace, we do as we please.

Hearts Intertwined in Truth

In a garden of giggles, we plant the seeds,
Twisting vines whisper secrets, indeed.
With laughter we barter, a joke for a smile,
Filling the air with warmth all the while.

Like socks on a line, truth hangs in the breeze,
What's real gets a chuckle, with humor that teases.
We dance on the roots, in this chaotic space,
A tangle of hearts, a comedy chase.

So let's prune the doubts with a snip and a slice,
Sprinkling puns like water, oh isn't it nice?
As we twirl through the path where the jesters convene,
Bound in hilarity, where joy's evergreen.

Together we blossom, bright and absurd,
In the foliage of friendship, each glance is a word.
Through the jumbles and jests, we're tightly knit,
In this patchwork of laughter, we never quit!

The Conduit of Clarity

A pipe full of banter, with giggles that flow,
We pipe in the truth, let the chuckles bestow.
With tales that are silly, yet not far from real,
We gather our thoughts, a strange merry wheel.

As clarity dances like shadows at noon,
We juggle with nonsense, a whimsical tune.
Each twist is a riddle, each turn is a jest,
In the fountain of laughter, we find our best rest.

Brimming with humor, we sip like fine wine,
Pouring out wisdom like cheese on a vine.
With every bright giggle, the clouds shape and shift,
In this conduit of clarity, smiles are the gift.

A splash here and there, truth sloshing about,
In this wacky canal, we don't live in doubt.
For what's clear is that laughter can light up the dark,
And in this fine conduit, joy hits the mark!

Cultivating Understanding Amidst Perception

In a garden of thoughts, we sprinkle some fun,
Nurturing ideas, under the sun.
Weeding out worries, planting some laughs,
With every bright joke, we sharpen our paths.

Twisted ideas sprout, like vines on a wall,
But sharing a chuckle breaks down every tall.
Through silliness woven, understanding does grow,
In the soil of our hearts, truths start to glow.

We water them gently with friendship and cheer,
Wait for the blooms of perspective to appear.
As we dance through confusion on laughter's stage,
We'll harvest some wisdom with each silly page.

In this playful garden, let's cultivate care,
With seeds of compassion, let's tend to our share.
For every bright chuckle helps knowledge to sprout,
In this realm of connection, let's giggle it out!

The Swinging Lantern of Honesty

A lantern of laughter swings in the night,
Casting shadows of truth, oh what a sight!
With flickering giggles illuminating the way,
We find our lost truths in the quirkiest play.

Each light-hearted jest, a beacon so bright,
Guides us through riddles, making wrongs feel right.
As we sway in the breeze, with dance not so grave,
In the glow of our honesty, we misbehave.

Round and round we spin, like kids at a fair,
With lanterns of laughter, we float in the air.
We illuminate shadows, allow quirks to shine,
In this swinging ensemble, our hearts intertwine.

So let's hold up our lanterns, let honesty beam,
With humor and truth, we'll venture and dream.
As the night gets late, we wink at the stars,
In this whimsical space, we're never too far!

Nature's Honest Lines

In the garden, gossip flows,
Between the blooms, the truth bestows.
A flower whispers, 'Don't you dare,'
While the sun beams down with radiant flair.

The bees buzz loud, they've no disguise,
Sipping nectar, sharing lies.
'The tulip's taller!' the daisies cry,
Yet they all know that blooms can't fly.

The trees shake hands with the breeze,
In secret talks about the bees.
Leaves can't keep their stories straight,
As squirrels debate their dinner plate.

So wander 'midst the flora's cheer,
Where honest chatter blooms each year.
From roots to leaves, they sing aloud,
In Nature's heart, you'll find the crowd.

Vines Looping Through Light

Vines twist and twirl, in sunlight they sway,
Murmuring tales of their wild play.
'I tangled you up!' one vine will boast,
While the other giggles, 'You missed the toast!'

Grapes have juicy secrets, they jump with glee,
'Watch out for that bee, he's sipping on me!'
The sunbeams laugh, while shadows tease,
As laughter dances on the wandering breeze.

Each leaf thinks it's quite the star,
But the moon just chuckles from afar.
'You're green but wise,' it sings in jest,
While the flowers argue on who's the best.

So spiral with the vines, take a chance,
Join their fun, and join the dance.
In nature's loop, the laughter climbs,
Amid the whims and leafy rhymes.

The Arbor of Unspoken Thoughts

Beneath the boughs where shadows play,
Squirrels ponder all the day.
'What if nuts could talk?' one cries,
While the other winks with twinkling eyes.

The branches creak with every laugh,
As thoughts weave in a leafy path.
'What's that you're hiding in your nest?'
'Just my secrets!' comes a playful jest.

The twilight swoops with a gentle sway,
While owls hoot wisdom, strange yet gay.
'Who's the wisest?' they all converse,
While crickets chirp, oh what a verse!

So linger here, where giggles meet,
In the arbor's shade, life feels sweet.
Where unspoken thoughts burst into light,
And every secret takes its flight.

The Fragrant Path of Candor

On a fragrant path, scents entwine,
Where honesty blooms in every line.
'That rose is red, but watch out, friend,'
Says a daisy dreaming, 'it has a bend!'

The herbs whisper riddles, fresh and bright,
While thyme tells tales of a surprising flight.
Basil protests, 'I'm the best cook!'
Olive nods, 'It's all in the look!'

'What's blooming over there?' the peonies ask,
While the violets giggle, 'Oh, what a task!'
As petals coordinate a fashion show,
With each little bud trying to steal the glow.

So stroll this path, and take a whiff,
Of nature's humor, and a happy skiff.
Where scents reveal what words can't say,
In laughter's embrace, we find our way.

Blossoms of Bold Enlightenment

In a garden where thoughts can bloom,
Ideas twist like a squirrel in a room.
With laughter and giggles, the petals sway,
As wisdom dances in a silly ballet.

A bee buzzes jokes, oh what a delight!
Pollinating puns, from morning till night.
Each blossom unfolds with a quirk and a grin,
Unlocking the secrets, let the fun begin!

The flowers gossip about the bee's latest scheme,
Turning serious moments into a daydream.
With sunlight and humor, they bask in the glow,
Letting their merry little spirits flow.

So pluck off a petal, let laughter ensue,
For every plucky bud whispers something new.
In this vibrant patch of wisdom so bright,
We find joy in the journey, and that feels just right.

The Tangles of True Expression

Words weave and wobble, like noodles on a plate,
Each twist and turn makes the meaning wait.
A string of laughter, a hint of surprise,
Expressing the truth with a wink of the eyes.

Tales spin like yarn in a cat's playful claw,
Tangled and messy, they break every law.
But in every twist there's a funny refrain,
In the chaos of telling, we have much to gain!

A parrot repeats, in a squawk so sincere,
Telling the truth with a side of good cheer.
The colors of language can sometimes confound,
But wrapped in a jest, it's where joy can be found.

So gather the blunders, the flops, and the slips,
For each awkward moment is where laughter trips.
In the tangle of words, let your spirit be free,
The truth can be funny; just wait and you'll see.

Beyond the Veil of Deceit

Peeking through curtains, where fibs often play,
Lies wear silly masks, oh what a display!
With a wink and a nod, they prance on the stage,
For the truth needs a break, it's locked in a cage.

Behind every ruse is a rubber chicken joke,
Slipping on truths, we all start to poke.
A magician appears with a poof and a grin,
As he tries to convince us that lying's a win!

But laughter is strong; it unveils all the tears,
It dances through shadows, confronting our fears.
So let's tickle the fabric, let's stretch every lie,
For the truth in this mess can soar and can fly!

Beyond the deceits, amidst giggles and fun,
We find that the truth can't be outdone.
So toss out the fables, unleash all your glee,
In the land beyond falseness, we all can be free.

Shadows of the Untruthful

In corners where whispers put on a disguise,
Shadows lurk behind in their clever reprise.
They giggle and chuckle at stories they weave,
Making a mockery of what we believe.

A shadow once claimed it could dance in the light,
But tripped on its tale, oh what a sight!
With a flurry of movement and a flap of a wing,
Untruths take flight, like a songbird they sing.

They mingle and jive, tickling truth with a joke,
Crafting a farce with every elbow poke.
Yet under their layers, there's sparkle and charm,
Hidden beneath, there's no need for alarm.

So let's spin a yarn, make shadows perform,
In this theater of silliness, we'll break every norm.
For even the untruthful can give us a break,
When laughter unravels the stories they make.

Lattice of Life's Secrets

Life's a jigsaw, all askew,
Pieces fitting, just not you.
Whispers float on breezy nights,
Silly secrets, all in sight.

Jokes behind the garden wall,
Gossip thrives where shadows fall.
We laugh at paths we've had to tread,
While tripping over what we said.

Roots entwined, they dance and sway,
Who knew truths could lead astray?
Underneath a grapevine vine,
Conspiracies in every line.

In this maze of green and brown,
We wear smiles, we don't frown.
Life's tall tales, a funny jest,
With every crack, we're truly blessed.

Threads of Honest Reflection

Beneath a loom where stories spin,
Threads get tangled, let's begin.
I try to weave a tale so bright,
But lose the plot by sheer delight.

Socks and ties, they fight for space,
Fashion don'ts in the wrong place.
Stray strands giggle, hide and seek,
Poking fun at every peak.

Tangled truths with lots of flair,
Quirky twists, woven with care.
Each yarn a flag, too loud to hide,
A vibrant mess, this tangled ride.

Pull one thread, watch them bounce,
Chasing laughter, what a flounce!
In this fabric, errors are gold,
Life's stitched stories, bright and bold.

Garden of Genuine Insights

In the garden of wacky dreams,
We plant ideas with silly themes.
Watered well with laughter's rain,
Harvest jokes and wise refrain.

Weeds of doubt don't stand a chance,
They trip and fall in a funny dance.
Sunflowers nod, with knowing grins,
As secrets sprout from all our sins.

Beneath the blooms, we dig for gold,
Finding humor in tales retold.
Butterflies flutter, whisper sweet,
In this garden, life's a treat.

With every root that bends and sways,
We gather giggles in the sun's rays.
A pie of truths, all baked with glee,
In this garden, we are free.

Arbors of Authenticity

Underneath the leafy shade,
We craft truths that can't be swayed.
Laughter echoes through the trees,
As we share tales, with silly tease.

Branches sway, with secrets bare,
You'll find the truth hiding where.
A bird will chirp a funny line,
While squirrels argue, oh so fine.

The trunk holds stories of old fights,
Knots and turns in gleeful sights.
Under this roof of bark and bloom,
We crack jokes and banish gloom.

In the whispers of the leaves,
Lies dissolve, the heart believes.
So let's toast with lemonade,
In this shade, let joy cascade.

Roots of Sincere Connection

In a garden where friendships sprout,
Giggles and chuckles dance about.
Like clumsy vines, they intertwine,
A bond grows stronger, oh so fine.

Beneath the surface, they wiggle and sway,
Tickling the roots at the end of the day.
A knot of laughter, a playful tease,
Friends share secrets with the greatest ease.

In shade of humor, we plant our glee,
Watered with jokes shared over tea.
When storms may come and winds may blow,
We hold each other; we're in the know.

So let us nurture this curious vine,
With shared laughter and some silly wine.
Roots of connection, deep and wide,
In this garden, there's joy to abide.

The Dwelling of Inner Knowledge

In the attic of thoughts, dust bunnies play,
In corners of wisdom, the shadows do sway.
A couch made of cushions, funny and bright,
We lounge in truth, till the morning light.

With googly eyes on a picture frame,
We ponder the secrets, but none feel the same.
Truth sits grinning, wearing a hat,
It whispers softly, 'Can you handle that?'

Between giggles and snorts, we discover the deal,
That wisdom is wacky, and often surreal.
In this quirky dwelling, full of delight,
We bounce off the walls, chuckling through the night.

So let us reside, in this haven of cheer,
Where knowledge is funny, and laughter is near.
In the dwelling of thought, we'll find what we seek,
With a wink from the wise, and a giggle so sleek.

Secrets in the Garden of Thought

In the garden of thought, where ideas bloom,
Silly notions giggle, create a fun room.
Petals of wisdom, all bright and absurd,
Share secrets with bees that hum and stir.

Underneath blossoms, deep underground,
Whispers of madness are joyfully found.
A carrot of wisdom, a radish with flair,
In this garden of giggles, we have not a care.

Frolicking frogs in the lily pad pond,
Croak out the truth, of this we're so fond.
With mulch of laughter, we dig and we play,
Planting wild thoughts, in the sun's golden ray.

So come, wander here, with your hat on askew,
Where secrets are silly, and blossoms are too.
In the garden of thought, let's twirl and we'll prance,
Finding the joy, in our wild, wacky dance.

The Shell of Honest Emotions

In a shell on the beach, emotions reside,
Waves of laughter crash, like a merry tide.
With a splash of honesty, a twist of the sea,
We peek inside, what a sight to see!

A crab of confusion, scuttles away,
While clams share their secrets, in a funny way.
Starfish of kindness, flapping their arms,
These shells of emotion, hold many charms.

With sand of sincerity, we build and we play,
Chasing our feelings, like children, we sway.
In shells of honesty, we find little glee,
Laughing together, oh so carefree.

So gather your shells, from the shore's gentle sweep,
Each one holds laughter, memories to keep.
In the shell of emotions, let's frolic with pride,
As waves of honest joy, crash side by side.

Framework of the Heart

In the garden of my chest, quite a sight,
Humor blooms, bursting with delight.
A squirrel rides a merry-go-round,
While whispers of joy in laughter abound.

When love's blueprint gets slightly twisted,
Funny how our dreams get unlisted.
Accidental hugs, a misplaced hat,
We laugh and dance, oh, imagine that!

Blueprints change with a sneeze or two,
And every mishap makes something new.
Why did the chicken cross the road?
To find a rhyme for a silly ode!

In the sketches of silly love's design,
We find our mess can spark the divine.
So here's to the joy in each little glitch,
In this framework of the heart, we find our niche!

Pathways of Pure Perception

Through winding roads of thought I wander,
With every step, my socks still ponder.
Why did the cat join the dance class?
To learn how to step without a pass!

Stars twinkle just right, oh what a show,
While I stumble over my own shadow.
Grasshopper wisdom on a slide,
Warns me, don't let the fun subside!

With thoughts like butterflies in full flight,
One lands on my nose, what a silly sight!
Is that a poet or just me sneezing?
In verses absurd, there's joy displeasing!

Chasing ideas down random lanes,
I giggle at the mischief of my brain's trains.
In this labyrinth of giggles and glee,
I strut through perception, wild and free!

Branches of Unveiled Understanding

Underneath the meme tree, I sit still,
Each branch holds knowledge, oh what a thrill!
A squirrel debates a wise old crow,
Who wins the argument? No one knows!

Leaves rustle with gossip, truths gone wild,
As the trees tease like a mischievous child.
What's the secret of life's great lore?
It's mostly about how to snore, and score!

A branch falls flat, with a comical thunk,
On the head of a scholar who's quite a funk.
He mutters, "I thought I'd find the truth,"
But all he got was a crack forsooth!

Yet in the branches, we laugh and glide,
Amidst the wisdom, let joy abide.
For in the shade of pure understanding,
Life's peculiar quirks are always demanding!

The Spire of Unspoken Realities

High atop the silly spire I climb,
With thoughts that wobble and perfectly rhyme.
A juggler tosses life's small secrets,
While a mime misinterprets all the receipts!

The view is quirky, clouds shaped like cats,
Who knew wisdom came from silly chats?
An owl hoots jokes from its perch up high,
Just trying to figure out why pigs can fly!

In this lofty space of unspoken fun,
Laughter echoes, and we've just begun.
Why do we fear the truth's great fall?
When giggles and grins can conquer all!

So let my spire reach the stars overhead,
With a wiggle and a laugh, I may be misled.
In this realm of truths left unspun,
Life's comedic dance leaves no one outrun!

Whispers Among the Vines

In the garden, secrets played,
The grapes giggled in a cascade.
A squirrel danced, oh so spry,
While birds debated the pie in the sky.

The sun winked at a shady plot,
Where herbs plotted a culinary hotshot.
Frogs in top hats sang their tune,
Dreaming of feasts under the moon.

Lettuce argued, 'We're quite right,'
While tomatoes blushed at a rumor's slight.
Bumblebees buzzed a jolly jest,
Of flowers' fashion—who wore the best?

Amidst the fun, a truth was spun,
In laughter's weave, the day was won.
As veggies joined in a silly spree,
The garden burbled with glee!

Shadows in the Garden

Beneath the boughs, where shadows prance,
Lettuce whispered in a trance.
A gnome grinned, with mischief keen,
Plotting with mushrooms, oh what a scene!

The sun peeked through, throwing glances,
While daisies blushed, waltzing in dances.
A bumblebee, in a tuxedo, roamed,
Claiming the flowers as his home.

In this space where giggles bloom,
A rake and a shovel planned their doom.
Digging for secrets, they tripped and fell,
Uncovering worms with stories to tell.

As day turned to dusk, the laughter grew,
With shadows blending in a silly stew.
In the garden, with all its quirk,
Every bloom, a joke, a timeless work!

Unraveling the Hidden Path

Down the lane where pumpkins roll,
Chickens gathered for a stroll.
They clucked and laughed, a comical crew,
Plotting to bake a pie or two.

As carrots sneezed, what a sight!
A breeze carried puns in delight.
The path twisted, with humor rife,
Leading to mischief and garden strife.

On this lane, a hedgehog pondered,
While roses giggled, quite flabbergasted.
A sign read, "Beware of the prickle!"
Yet laughter echoed—oh what a trickle!

At the end of this quirky way,
A party awaited, come join, hooray!
With frolic and fun under the sun,
The garden's secret had just begun!

Secrets Beneath the Arbors

Under arches, where shadows play,
Vines shared gossip, come what may.
The lilies rolled their frilly eyes,
When daisies flaunted their own surprise.

A rabbit claimed he'd won the race,
Though he tripped in a frantic chase.
The squirrels chuckled, tails a-twist,
In this garden of humor, none could resist.

The old oak sighed, its branches shook,
As mischievous winds wrote a funny book.
With every rustle, a chuckle soared,
In secrets shared, laughter roared.

As twilight fell on this jovial scene,
The stars peeked in, bright and keen.
Beneath the arbors, with mirth and cheer,
Life's little truths felt strangely clear!

Roots of Revelation

Deep in the ground where secrets sleep,
Worms tell tales while the crickets peep.
Each root a story, a laugh to share,
Even the daisies think they're rare.

Beneath the soil, the jokes take flight,
A pun from the tulip, what a delight!
The carrots giggle with glee and mirth,
While potatoes hide, claiming they're worth.

The vines share gossip, twirling about,
Whispering truths, never in doubt.
The radishes chuckle, oh what a sight,
With leaves that dance in pure delight.

So join the party, don't miss the fun,
Among the greenery, we are all one.
In this wacky garden, come have a blast,
With roots and their humor, a friendship cast!

The Structure of Serene Reality

In a garden plot of wiggly lines,
The hedges plot mischief, share their designs.
The fence is a jester, full of jest,
While weeds wear crowns, thinking they're best.

Concrete thoughts grow where flowers twirl,
Each petal laughing, giving a whirl.
The sun makes puns, oh so absurd,
As shadows giggle, not saying a word.

Paths paved with laughter, in every nook,
The bench tells stories, come take a look!
Seating wise frogs who read from a book,
They'll crack you up, just take a hook.

So come explore this wacky place,
Where structure bends in silly grace.
Reality's true, it's all in your head,
With joy in the garden, let worries shred!

Petals of Profound Trust

A daisy sways with a wink and a nod,
Trusting the sun to give her a prod.
While roses giggle, secretly pink,
Whispering secrets before flowers shrink.

Petals catch laughter as it skips by,
With bees doing ballet, oh my, oh my!
The lilacs nod as if in on the game,
When tulips schmooze, never feeling lame.

A root may trip you, but that's just fun,
In a meadow of laughs, we're all number one.
Trust in the blooms, they know how to play,
With petals of joy brightening the way.

So let's dance in this colorful spree,
With trust in the blooms and silly glee.
In a world where petals send chuckles and cheer,
We grow together, year after year!

Revelation in the Garden

In a patch of green where giggles grow,
Each seed unfolds with a charming glow.
The carrots proclaim, "We taste divine!"
While peas just grin and fold their design.

The cucumbers laugh, rolling on the ground,
With jokes so corny, they astound!
Zucchini's the king, lush and so bright,
He reigns with humor, a real delight.

Sprouts bring wisdom as they peek and peep,
With whispered punchlines that never sleep.
A cabbage winks, wearing a bow,
In this garden of laughter, friendships grow!

From flowers to veggies, all have a part,
In this funny garden that's close to the heart.
Join the revelry, no need to refrain,
In the laughter of nature, we'll never complain!

Beneath the Green Canopy

Under the leaf, a squirrel did dance,
Chasing his tail, lost in a trance.
A bird called out, "Is that a snack?"
But it was just a pinecone, what a whack!

Sunbeams peeked through, like giggling sprites,
While ants marched on, in perfect sights.
A butterfly sneezed, then took to the skies,
Painting the air with colorful lies.

The breeze told jokes, so light and spry,
As I laughed along, asking, "Oh my?!"
Nature's humor, quite the show,
Revealing truths in a wacky flow.

In the Maze of Tender Leaves

In a maze of green, I lost my way,
Chasing a rabbit, he said, "Not today!"
A snail waved slowly, with a sly little grin,
"Life's not a race, but oh what a spin!"

The wind whispered secrets that tickled my ear,
While the flowers giggled, "We've nothing to fear!"
A chubby little toad croaked out a pun,
"Why did the fly just hop and run?"

A hedge hog snickered, rolled up in a ball,
"Nature's a joke, now that's not all!"
With every twist and turn, I found myself lost,
In laughter's embrace, I'd pay any cost.

Harvesting the Fruits of Awareness

In the orchard bright, fruits hung with glee,
"Pick me, pick me!" they shouted at me.
A pear made a face, oh what a sight,
And an apple replied, "I'm just ripe for the bite!"

Beneath the branches, a debate took flight,
"Mangoes are better!" "No, berries are right!"
A fruit fly buzzed, "Why not both, my friends?"
"Let's celebrate now, let's put this to bends!"

An orange rolled over, laughing so loud,
"I'm juicy and sweet, come join the crowd!"
With every pluck, a giggle would bloom,
Nature's buffet, dispelling the gloom.

Nature's Secrets Unfold

Amidst the ferns, a mystery spun,
A hedgehog was plotting, "I'm going to run!"
With each little rustle, secrets revealed,
Nature's own laughter, beautifully sealed.

A critter with glasses was reading a leaf,
"Words can be funny, just beyond belief."
The trees started chuckling, roots in a tangle,
"Follow the whispers, don't let them strangle!"

The daisies joined in, with giggles galore,
"Watch out for bees, they can really ignore!"
But a bee just buzzed, "I'm here for the taste,
Nature's great feasts can't go to waste!"

With laughter dispersed through the breeze all around,
Nature's secrets unfolded, joy to be found!

www.ingramcontent.com/pod-product-compliance
Lightning Source LLC
Chambersburg PA
CBHW051634160426
43209CB00004B/645